THE FLESH OF ICE

01 02 03 04 05 28 27 26 25 24

Caitlin Press Inc.
3375 Ponderosa Way
Qualicum Beach, BC V9K 2J8
www.caitlinpress.com

Cover art and design by Tania Willard
Text design by Vici Johnstone
Printed in Canada

Caitlin Press Inc. acknowledges financial support from the Government of Can-
ada and the Canada Council for the Arts, and the Province of British Columbia
through the British Columbia Arts Council and the Book Publisher's Tax Credit.

The flesh of ice / Garry Gottfriedson.
Gottfriedson, Garry, 1954- author.
Canadiana 2024036791X | ISBN 9781773861579 (softcover)
LCGFT: Poetry.
LCC PS8563.O8388 F54 2024 | DDC C811/.6—dc23

The Flesh of Ice

Poetry by
Garry Gottfriedson

Caitlin Press

Dedicated to le estcwicwéẏ
'The Missing'

This book is dedicated to all of those who attended the Kamloops Indian Residential School (KIRS) and all residential schools in Canada. It is a special tribute to the 215+ Le estcwicwéẏ (the missing) found in May 2021 at KIRS.

Contents

Granny—42

Mom—43

Agnes—44

Dolly—45

Karly—46

Mia—47

Margaret—48

Dessa—49

Charlotte—50

Shae—51

Rita—52

Mary—53

Ethel—54

Alice—55

Alexa—56

Joanne—57

Katherine—58

Brenda—59

Sandra—60

Lucy—61

Maggie—62

Mariyah—63

Millie—64

Nettie—65

Lacy—66

Pearl—68

Rosa—69

Sadie—70

Susan—71

Laila—72

When Yellow Leaves Detach—73

Dad—74

Adam—75

Zach—76

Albert—77

George—78

Angus—79

Michael—80

Andrew—81

Bobby—82

Timmy—83

Clem—84

Eric—85

Cody—86

Cam—87

Ryan—88

Boyd—89

Gus—90

Darcy—91

Henry—92

Joe—93

Keegan—94

Prologue

By Celia Haig-Brown

Kamloops Indian Residential School (KIRS): the stories my friends and their parents told me changed this white woman's life, my understandings of Canada, and sent me on a trajectory of trying to respond with love to what I had heard and could not unhear. My master's thesis was published in 1988 as *Resistance and Renewal: Surviving the Indian Residential School*. It contained extended excerpts from testimonies of thirteen former students of KIRS. Those stories went out into the world and shocked some and affirmed the experiences of so many others. Then in 2021, the 215+ Le estcwicwéy̓ (the missing) called me back to rethink what I thought I knew. And called the world to attention to the schools and their colonial agenda.

Garry Gottfriedson and his family, especially his mother, Mildred—who I always knew as Millie—have generously built on the lessons my family taught me, about what it means to be a Canadian living on Indigenous lands often illegally and always unethically. I am honoured that Garry invited me to write this prologue.

In 1975, I was teaching English in Kamloops Senior Secondary School, as it was called at the time. One of six classes was a group of thirty-six Grade Tens—thirty-five teenage boys and one girl. She was strong, mature, and managed to ignore the shenanigans around her. The rest of the class was made up of cowboys and "Indians," hockey players and farmers and a few poets and literary scholars. Yes, even at that age.

The thing about teaching high school is that you can never actually know what a student is learning. Sometimes if you are very lucky, years later, you may get to know something of what was happening there. Little did I know that one of those "Indian" cowboys was listening closely and internalizing the power of poetry. Maybe it was Richard Brautigan's *Memoirs of Jesse James* that won him over: "My teachers could easily have ridden with Jesse James/for all the time they stole from me." Garry Gottfriedson was in that class. Much later he told me what it meant to him.

And now we all benefit perhaps from the lessons he learned there and definitely from all that has followed. In this book, his potent words bring us into the centre of what KIRS—church and state, priests and nuns and government agents—has meant to so many Indigenous children and their families. The lasting impact of Canada's commitment to Christianize and civilize the original peoples of this land are evident on every page. The lasting impact of KIRS on Garry and on the people whose stories he gives to us are haunting, relentless and, at the same time, somehow hold the possibility of regeneration in the truths they bring. Tsqelmucwílc: the return to being human.

In 2021, when the 215+ Le estcwicwéý were brought to light, a former student of the Port Alberni Residential School reconnected with me. Randy Fred of the Tseshaht Nation was the publisher who accepted *Resistance and Renewal* all those years ago when a university press rejected it for being "one-sided." "Celia," he said, "we have to revisit *Resistance and Renewal.*" Despite my protestations—"Randy, there are so many Indigenous authors who are writing now"—he simply said he would contact the publisher and get back to me.

What a wonderful task Randy assigned us. What an opportunity to revisit the earlier work, to give names to those who had shared their lives with me at a time when anonymity was required by the university, to open the pages for those who would add to the original testimonies sharing their resistance, their survival, and their ongoing work toward justice. Garry agreed to write the prologue, Randy the preface and *Tsqelmucwílc*, another gift from Garry, became the title of this new version launched on the driveway outside KIRS on September 30, 2022, National Day for Truth and Reconciliation.

Relationship, responsibility, respect, and reciprocity: my take on the Four R's originally proposed by Cree scholar Verna Kirkness and her colleague Ray Barnhardt. Garry asking me to write the prologue for *The Flesh of Ice* renews our relationship, allowing it to grow ever deeper. In what I see as an act of reciprocity, I express my respect for all the work he continues to do and my responsibility to articulate the meanings I find here.

Over the last months, Garry shared some of these poems with me as he worked on them. As I sat in my condo in Toronto, he drew me into the rooms with the children—the tears, the hunger, the cracking of bone, the slicing of skin, the secrets, the bent knees, the bruised hearts, the crushing loneliness. Words pointing clearly to the source: pope, priest, nun, church, vatican, oblates, catholic, penance, contrition, sacrament, confession, rosary, bibles and the list goes on. 215+ again and again. And then the names: those human beings who suffered and those who punished. What is about names that makes it all so hyper-real? That brings those deeds to life? That tears and breaks over me?

And yet, woven around the pain of those lost in so many ways are the resistance and the beauty of the teachings that sustained the children and the adults they became. The devastating and the uplifting intertwined. And always love shines through: parents, grandparents, the wind, the water and the land. Sometimes erotic and sometimes longing, and always palpably real: rains chiming against panes; berries hitting bucket bottoms.

Drawing on the work of the late legal scholar Patricia Monture-Angus, I find fitting words for this book and for the former students of KIRS: first we were victims, then we were survivors and now we are warriors. Those warriors have now become teachers—teachers for those who learn to listen to the voices in this book. Garry's words deepen the gift—the learning, the passing on of knowledge in a way that moves the body, heart and mind.

Strong Winds

wind speaks
grey storms
yellow horizons await
low rumbling whispers

the names of the 'missing'
loudly sweeping across
secwepemcétkwe ell secwepemcúlucw
secwépemc waters and secwépemc land
responsive raw release
winds pushing waves
tumbling onto solid land
washing bones ashore
spines and femurs rattling rhythms
exhaling
windy truths

In Your Canada — A Thousand and Counting

a dress, a red dress, a thousand more dresses
suspended from crucifixes

tribute to the Holy Trinity:
daughter, mother, grandmother

condemned by the church
concealed by the government

caught in black clouds weeping
thunder breaking sky blue

a single rainbow drops from heaven
bridging souls to something much higher

than the sins of mortal men
hell-bent on killing brown women

as if hysterectomies, rape and murder
were not enough punishment

warranted by a civilized society
that honours genocide

all encapsulated by a single photo
a dress, a red dress, a thousand more dresses

215 — Kamloops Indian Residential School (KIRS)

perhaps 215
is a used number counted
forwards or backwards infinitely
never debated within the doctrine of discovery

perhaps 215
is teatime for the pope
as he scrolls names of the missing
in alphabetical order, unapologetic in toxic silence

perhaps 215
is one by one tears drip, dripping at unmarked graves
because survivors avoided the pope's wrath
and were too young to understand selection

perhaps 215
are jagged rocks stuck in throats
muffling fabrications, denying genocide
choked up around oak tables in papal chambers

perhaps 215
are hearts astonished
crying in kind honesty
wishing they could only count to zero

KIRS Curriculum

teach children
domestic skills

like how to hate
the opposite sex

like pruning trees
to blossom dysfunction

like planting seeds
to sprout self-loathing

like learning the word of god
on bent knees pleases priests

like discovering death 215 times
multiplied infinitely

Counting

215 names of children
concealed
within vatican ledgers
fortified and preserved
by rightist rogues
exploring
experimental rituals

like rape
like sodomy
like impregnations
like abortions
like public humiliations
like beatings
like starvation

sanctified by the pope
authorized by the queen

215 families affected
and counting

A Blow

a blow
a creeping blow
a lurid cracking-the-skull blow
a flesh-eating raw blow
a low black heartless blow
a violent bruising-the-heart blow
a directly aimed solid blow
straight at the origin of culture and identity
                    below

An Unholy Act

chopping off fingers
stealing for starving
kids imprisoned
might satisfy cruel
catholic intentions

slicing skin and bone
a blade at a time
to show example
and offer penance
was an unholy act
regardless

contrition and sacrament
does not erase
wrongdoings
no matter how close
one is to god

shame and guilt
slays anything good
but believing in hope
brings peace of mind

regardless, what good does it do
on empty bellies and forever reminders
like chopped off fingers?

For Now

devoted blue eyes
mischievously scoping
angelic innocence
gender has no bearing

zoning in on playtime
the harmless child is unattuned
to this game heavy
with lifelong consequences

but anything goes
in the confession box
with a rosary in hand
ten our fathers

does the trick
in the absence of god
besides, who else witnesses
the devil's deeds

but a devil himself... for now

Soft Prayer

soft prayer
silent heart
coincidence?

in a deaf heaven

it is sinful
to suffer alone
shamed and powerless

in a deaf heaven

cold men of god sipping
hot tea, nibbling croissants
thread rotting rosaries

in a deaf heaven

the vatican is heavy
but mourning survivors
carry the weight

all the way to a deaf heaven

The Political Other

the political 'other'

male
female
something in between
a combination of the two
a combination of many

words
forms
views
values
beliefs

an amalgam of 'other' scruples
the political other

The Blood Quantum Other

on which 'other' should you decide?
indigenous? white?
decolonized? colonized?
Secwepemctsín? english?

when I speak
I speak in mixed
blood 'other' tongue
a combination of tones
blending shades
creating beige

let's talk about the 'mix'
white paper policy mix
desire or desirable mix
blood mix
quantum mix
a cosmopolitan hybrid machine mix
diluted brown mix
external norms mix
tantalizing mix
exotic rez boy / city boy combo mix

constantly at war...

We Count Our Years by the Budding Leaves in Spring

qwinc te swult?
how many winters?
the Old Ones ask

time measured
by melting snow
and the return
of new leaves
breaking through
the spring sun

our ancestors speaking in our blood
jabbing our memories living in our skins
reminding us to bury autumn death
to look for the budding leaves in spring

cycles as old as the moon

My Body as Storyteller

my body
as storyteller
breaks
elegantly
215 times
repeatedly
infinitely

sometimes
it's a trashy
love story
or
a narrative
beautifully
scribed

sometimes
the book's spine cracks
under the weight of words
beaten
and bent
into something
more
worthy
than the self-
inflicted pain
of others

sometimes,
the plot drives
meaning
towards the protagonist
rising above the odds
215 times
repeatedly
infinitely

Texting Dead Loves

compulsive notions
resurrecting
dead love

fanatical ideas
useless
in this state

scrolling
out-of-service
telephone numbers

fingers flipping
iphone
directories

swooping
memory's
archives

soul stuffing
self-inflicted
lateral violence

angst
chiming insistent
hope

dull headspace
fixated and full
of compunction

logic
doesn't thrive
in the heart

a mouth full
of strawberry love
spat out

but the soul
has compelling needs
juxtaposed to rationality

fraught fingers
argue to text
or not to text

ruthless
joisting
forwards and backwards

the mind fancies things
real or not
destabilized

self-talk or
saxophone drones
reeling in names of ghosts

smashing notes
on cement floors
when the screen is blank

crushing
riffs on rocks
making sad sand

crafting
dead love
ballads

lapping .
against ears and hearts
making fingers bleed

it is tough
strumming rocks
instead of guitars

dial that number
neurotic
determinations

will answer your call
hunger
rots the bones

Dirty Love

eroticizing boys
arousing fantasy
the moment the predator sees
naked brown skin shining
brightness on the shoulders
the way the sun loosens its love
along the back, eyes digging
deeply into spines

the boy's gut knows
something is iniquitous
the overwhelming gnarling inside
acutely rendered the lack of understanding
a man's throbbing body
and way it moves
unknown to a child

it is calculated prowling
shaping movement
the sharpness in a predator's eyes
the hunter's attack
lips without a smile
the unzipping of pants

it is a boy's disorientation
confusion in the moment
blood rushing below the belt
the moment salty seas erupt
over the hunter's fat stomach
dripping onto the grey floor
creating puzzlement for his game

a chaotic world unfolding
for a boy's step into manhood
that incorruptibility is a child's possession
that vulnerability occurs
the moment men crave dirty love

Toothless

it's when
hard women become toothless
and soft men become women
resistance is paramount
215 times 215
children staked
to cement crucifixes
enduring the rise and fall
of residential schools
defenseless
against bibles
black robes and swinging rosaries
lambs for the slaughter
savoured in the priest's palate
devoured by pasty-faced nuns
carving a path
for drug dealing dogs dishing out
death warrants
an array of fentanyl funerals
betraying family q-time
crack
melting teeth
quick fix delusion
stopping blood
leaving
rope marks on necks
the old outliving the young
thickening realities
means resisting more
than an eagle feather in hand
boldly, keeping teeth gives reason
for chewing on things
and makes the voice vibrate with reason
but hardening soft men
is not an easy task
especially when women turn to stone

The Red Dress and White Picket Fence

he buried the red dress
he was shamed into wearing
by a woman whiter
than the paint-peeling picket fence
he nailed his status card to
while she dim-wittedly tacked
herself to the Centre Tree
creating harm

she thought she had spirit
calling herself 'mother'
but some thoughts are deceptive
like some women are childless
but still driven by privilege

instead of reality,
prayer was a fatal fixation
spikes protruding from her tongue
mesmerized by skin colour
obtuse to the obvious
and deaf to all sounds alive
'pretendian' mowed over her body
and she never felt anything

in his world, she was tolerated
even pitied for her soullessness
but all people have a place
some never know theirs
she reinforced her own
homelessness
in his motherland without honour
stripping him of his vocal cords
but he had keen vision
scripting history with paint brushes
as he raked his arms with knives
bleeding out naughty antiquity
using his magic

making good medicine
ripe and ready
to be tied to a dying fence
praising his mother's name
stamping her life on canvas
his bleeding arms transcended art
instead of death
because his mother was real

and beneath that erected fence
and that puddle of blood and paint
he sprawled an artificial lawn
weighted down with the heaviness
of imposter names, replacing them
with the names of his life-givers
removed from the red cloth
left to rot

Triangles

mirrors don't lie

reversing reflection
edging red
fear in the eyes
fingers nearly pressing
speed-dial on the cell
directly to your number
afraid of not knowing
if the call will be answered
texting is an option
but trepidation outweighs logic
deleting is a compulsive act
push the send arrow, be brave!

why procrastinate?

time has no pity
dream in the blue night, if it helps
you are alive in dreams
facing the Atlantic
calling your lover's name
salt filling your mouth
helpless at the shore's edge
your heart, a dry gulch coughing up
vulnerability

staring into the mirror

your name caught in the throat
a thousand miles inland
daydream moments
walking barefoot on gravel roads
still hearing
ocean roars between lovers
mountaintop winds
constructing triangles

stinging rock surfaces
stinging aging skin
a face without laughter
craving the sun
so far away in shady places
to protect burning eyes
caught in the lead of mirrors
tell the truth

forevermore

The Flesh of Ice

river's frozen face
gnarled and jammed
thick ice skin
clear and sharp
reflections
stagnant in winter
crisp
crunching
snow
echoing footsteps
215 times
tromping
deceptive intentions
from the dorms to the river
picks and crow bars
weighing shoulders down
numb hands
sculpting
icy surfaces
lifeless bodies
roll out of woolen blankets
plunder frigid water
and jam beneath the flesh of ice
faces with forgotten names
sinking, sinking

Tremors

fingers tracing
skin-scape
tremors
rising and falling
with the sun's slow sleep
and a lazy moon strolls
mountain silhouettes
creeping slowly
across the blue of night
juniper scent fills and lingers
the breath of nightfall
purging
the stillness of moon's yellow haze
blanketing bodies
heated by the moment
an insistent drumming within
heaving frames
solid and athletic
aflame
finger tracks trickling
sweaty spines
far off thunder
rumbling
beneath ribcages
deeply
echoing
along canyons and cliffs
soft waterfalls
pooling
bellies quivering an aching
desire
forevermore

Returning from School

when you return from KIRS
bruised and blue
optimism
barely
surviving
nonetheless, alive
calling your spirit
home
reminding you
your family still stands firm
open to the sun
waiting to blanket you

sage smoke adrift
rising from our cupped hands
sweeping a path
for your wandering feet
guided back to us
where you belong
where our people have always belonged
Secwepemcúlucw

remember our strength,
broken as it may be,
arises from the sage smoke and dust
of those who walked the same path
generations before
teaching us to dig deeply
into the sweetness of this land
baring our roots
tracking the hoof-prints of t́si7 – the deer
and making our way to setétkwe – the river
tossing salmon skeletons
back into the water
for these elements
carry the celebration of those
who once lived among us

and who have kept us resilient
despite destructive attempts to
expunge ck̓ultn – our way of being
and when you are crazy with confusion
your returning
signals
tsqelmucwílc – your return to becoming human
forevermore

Setétkwe – The River

setétkwe, the river
forever moving forward
never looking backward

her moving body
winding its way
along the skin of land
ancestors naming you

setétkwe, the river
forever moving forward
never looking backward

she is the architect
building clouds
weeping rain
making blood filling bodies

setétkwe, the river
forever moving forward
never looking backward

Water Is Life

our bodies are water
swimming in wombs
pulsing heartbeats
never to be taken
for granted

and at the right time
departure is inevitable

a women's song
a women's frame
positioning
to greet new life
the skin of land and sky

men standing guard
singing love lullabies
for mother and child

natural law
our way of life
soul-marking territory
voicing
ancestral names
never forgotten

blessing
and praying
for the newborns, and
for those yet to be born

our remembrance
water is life
spilled at birth
written from our blood

Granny

no one came
to our rescue

how could they?
law forbid it

so we dreamed
freedom

nestled in Granny's house
nibbling

fresh bannock
and strawberry jam

her soft touch
upon our heads

reassuring
her love lived

Mom

warned me
guided by wounds

"be careful son," she said
a damaged heart equals risky business

I listened carefully
and examined the scars

the epiphany of love
is seeing what you hear

and I see all of you
clearly

Agnes

was beautiful
and unsurprisingly graceful
in her natural environment

her grandmother rooted
Secwepemcúlucw into her bones
long before she attended KIRS

she arrived with the land's rhythm
pulsing in her blood and muscle
and then she learned to dance Mexican

because she had the look,
the transformation
considered civilized form

she was a showpiece
displayed in public
for pleasure and support

but it was a fun escape
from the nun's routine leg beatings
and father's stench

in the end, she returned
home setsínmes ell t̓iy
singing and dancing – still beautiful

Dolly

cried softly alone
hardening the traumatized child within

her illusion was cheap
tears dropping stones

her whimpers were thick
dirty sounds rolling off her thin tongue

thriving on the sorrow
and the ugly mess of others

until her belly ached
unrelenting disillusion

and there was nothing left
but integrity struggle

while dignity soul-wrapped her prey
and her cries were dry tears hitting cement

Karly

how many times will you try
to rip the Secwépemc out of me?

questioned Karly

understanding
the measurement of blood quantum
only justifies colonial mongrels

she knew

each conversation
rose her blood pressure
to the fullness of a Secwépemc heart

she repeated, "get over it!"

Mia

stood at the cement ledge
peering into Coal Harbour
her murky image swaying in the water
like a landmark
edging Canada Place in the August heat

she didn't care about that
her circumstance was hot conversation
for people accustomed to air-conditioning
bitching in rush hour
unattuned to pollution rising

we sat in the stale afternoon
amid the cars honking
witnessing her defiant gracefulness
mesmerized by her contemplation
men never really know a woman's sanctuary

we saw how her Indigenous skin lived in the sun
wrinkled lines, each a story of survival
her bones protruding aches
eyes focussed on the inevitable
dreaming of life before white men, perhaps…

"Mia is going to jump" I said
you replied, "No she won't,
she has a mango in her hand"
wealth attained by what others disvalue
I thought of the sadness she carried in her life

images never leaving the mind
a mango, a weather-torn hand, a woman, named Mia, appearing to jump
the way the sun bounced off of her brown skin on an August day
her Indigenous beauty deeply steeped and surviving in colonial rule
the way men are imperceptive to what is going on around them –
Canada place

Margaret

Margaret's days ended head crushed in beaten silly
seven years old and never knowing peace
she was alive in Susan's cruel smile
that cartoon-cat grin telling the
whole story without apology
without regret, after all,
she and Margaret lived
side-by-side on the
girls' side at KIRS
the difference
being Margaret
didn't live
long enough
to become
Susan

Dessa

was sharper
than her dad's
hunting knife

she bluntly stated
there is such a thing
as being too honest
for one's own good

her all-seeing eyes never lost
sight of targets
knowing truth is naked

her candid words
were not for the weak
tooting murky faces
or queens bent on drama

she claimed victimization
easily impresses others
shaped by fear

still her sober honesty
dangled in the conscience of others
telling lies to themselves
she never had a dull moment

Charlotte

moved from the KIRS dorms
to her husband's bedroom

learned to be a life-giver the hard way
expected ugly love from her man

instead, he built her a home
full of vibrant spaces and moving colour

knowing the sound of children
beckons the ancestors

and when she understood
she was not alone

residential school dorm memories
faded

like night sounds over-shadowing
creaking floors

Shae

witnessed the rain turn to snow
on that November day
returning an unforeseen text
that professed a long-awaited love

he was drawn to her natural rez beauty
fantasized hooks in her skin
bleeding out her soul
for him, while he lay in bed alone

the furnace rumbled deep growls
and reminding Shae of the first time
she heard an avalanche in the Roger's Pass
her heart filled with distress

aware that elements were alive
like the long and loud winters
deeply embedded in cold loneliness and fear
alert to settler mindset

she typed slushy words
"I have deep respect for your marriage"
December is not far away
even in the perfect marriage

Rita

embraced another winter passing
muscle memory fueling April rains
chiming against panes
home seemed far away

spring showers, like grandma's soft tears,
strumming songs during insensitive nights
she followed her song through longer days
calling for new life in the summer sun
lulling the slowness of cacti blooming
her voice, alive, shaking sage in gentle winds

she remembered berries hitting basket bottoms
filling birchbark bowls
carrying newfound memories into autumn
light-footed and light-hearted
over paths leading the way

she recalled grandma humming earth chants
echoing off the skin of fir and pines
calling back the names of forever places
and she found her way home

Mary

arose from the skids
in downtown east side
Vancouver shining light
sharing ancestral messages
walking amid piss-ridden streets

clear to her call
she returned to the rez
with unrefined answers

she never failed

alive with hope-seekers
returning to themselves
returning home
smashing bottles of holy water and shame

she, and they, arose from the abyss
between Chinatown and gastown
with arms and hearts punctured
but hands full of sage and fire
shining light

Ethel

was the youngest
sister of 10 siblings
and the last to go to KIRS

her parents' hearts broke
when she was hauled
off in a cattle truck

amid her peers
whose own hearts became locked
in the sound of rubber on gravel

dust consumed their breath
and tears burned
their love to ash

but Ethel never forgot
her duty was final
to her parents in old age

she returned home
cold and wrecked
still a child

mending her parents'
broken hearts
with the last of the cattle

left to die
in slaughterhouses
her lungs still full of dust

Alice

the oblates favoured
her fairness draping her insides

Alice was a pale-skinned babe
rosy cheeks and grey eyes that

circumvented
punishment

unlike her dark-skinned kin
starved and abused

bleeding
colonial disorder

from the inside out
for no perfect reason

nor for the greatest
achievement of civilized decree

the anointment
of a favourite child

depended
upon her whiteness

Alexa

crossed the line
onward to healing

deeply aware of
colonial aspiration

deuced in dirty
love and desire

she found true adoration
unexpectedly

bones to bones
spirit to spirit

the division between
death and life

perfect lines
merging

expectedly, she chose life
and never looked back

Joanne

your name
will be
spoken
by people
who don't
even know
you
in rooms
that you
will never
go in
becoming
a symbol of strength
where weakness blooms
tattoo this
in the hearts of girls
following
your name

Katherine

Katherine hid KIRS'
dirty secrets in her body
until they rotted her insides
diverting torment, transforming it
into raw fearlessness that cemented
the iron in her fists, the terror in her heart
because after all, it's only human to tell the truth
somehow, even if it takes years for the body to say so

Brenda

watched her house
fall apart
when she returned to the rez
not knowing what family was

dysfunction was the norm
for residential school kids
and it carried onto the rez
with accuracy and sharp consequences

ochre paint houses
cracked and peeled
decades of kiss and don't tell
concealment

blood exposed walls
stained for generations to see
dripping stories of worthlessness
handed down as modern Kiyoti stories

etched forevermore on brick tongues
hardly audible in a world painted white
but she found swelling words to recreate family
until death would do her part

Sandra

carried distress on her back
like all of the silk lining of men
she birthed into hatred and indignity
stitching angst into their spines
a needle and thread weaving
215 reasons to lash out
survival one stitch at a time
completing a garment
dyed with men's blood
one drop at a time

Lucy

as a teen, Lucy became
the rez boys' muse
monks and priests, too,
groomed her to endure
dirty love
at age eight, and at sixteen
she was homeless
surviving in rez slums
clustered around St. Joseph church
where rez boys were proficient
with what they learned at KIRS

although tarnished
like the beads and crucifix
hanging from the priests' neck,
Lucy died a pure woman at sixty-five

Maggie

pissed by the church steps
one time, in protest

and never looked back
as she walked past the graveyard

on her way to Indian Point
humming an old song

she learned
from grandmothers long gone

Maggie was known to do crazy things
but she knew who she was

despite scrubbing plank floors
and getting raped at KIRS

she called it 'doing time'
and was set free to other wolves

spending her time
by the river's edge

throwing salmon bones into the water
waiting for their return

and when they did
she sang Secwépemc songs

she knew the natural law
and pissing was just a small part of it

Mariyah

was pitch-perfect
singing Granny's ancestral songs

in the long days of summer
wandering tmicw – the earth

when the land was heavy
with rich and ripe berries

but that changed
at the residential school

when the hardened hand
of sister superior knocked

the sound of music
from Mariyah's soap-filled mouth

never to sing again
in the presence of the lord

but she still felt
the drum pounding

in Granny's heart
never forgetting that pitch

Millie

celebrated
resilience

bringing back alive
songs and dances

that lay long-time sleeping
from the land waiting

for the perfect voice
Secwepemcúlucw recognized

to resurrect the dust and memory
of ancestors watching from afar

her life was an act
of celebratory protest

a secret the church couldn't kill

Nettie

Nettie's hands were peeled
raw with calluses and crucifixes
doing time at KIRS

she scrubbed
the habits of nuns and priests
wrung out their sins

she returned to the rez
with her fingers dry of blood
and a heart full of forgiveness

Nettie was granny
to the rez orphans
and we felt her love

through her hands
once her heart started
pumping blood once again

Lacy

learned that she was a first
generation KIRS school survivor

oblivious to that experience
her heart was lovingly pure

and her uncles and aunties gave
her the gift of ckúltn – cultural teachings

Lacy lived in two worlds
showing it with soft eyes

she found love
far from the confinement of the rez

he was obtuse to the world
she derived from

she was open about her journey
but he only saw white clouds on the horizon

with gentle love
she spoke of storms and horses

"if you want to keep me
you've got to discover me

because I am obvious
on mountainsides

making my way
to clear creeks and rivers

taking cold water baths
to strengthen my spirit

naked in water and wind
listening for your name"

and when he didn't hear it
she escaped on horseback

wishing she was riding double
with sealed and cleansed souls

openly alive
she awaited discovery

Pearl

strapped and beaten before us
at KIRS, arms outstretched
weighted down with bibles
too heavy for the nuns to pack
and nailed to Pearl's hands
while blood oozed from her back,
a nun's revenge and Jesus' love
welting her skin and heart, head
hung in agony and bafflement
as if she were Mary Magdalene
instead of Jesus, not knowing a single
english word to appease sister mary
bernadette elated to offer her
services to church and country
as Pearl's family dug her grave

we were in grade three

Rosa

grew old before her time
at 16, she experienced
her grandparents' lifetime

her bent back burdened
the weight of the church
for the sake of her kin

she never complained
but her eyes spoke
clearly of that Kiyoti experience

and her heart hungered
for a time when Kiyoti
only spoke Secwepemctsín

sqepts, spring answered
and led her straight
into the arms of the Old Ones

Sadie

night built
burdens
upon Sadie's back

brick by brick
she carried
pieces of lives

always dreaming
new beginnings
etched in dense clay

dawn's rays beaming
weightless flight
and the density of kindness

others had shown
her in yesterday's sun
living to tell the story

repeatedly...

Susan

learned what
absolute hate was
because she knew nothing
else, surviving KIRS impaled love
and logic, and she was a survivor
but somewhere in that brick structure
the child died giving birth to horrific rage
that made torture and murder logical in her
mind, and Margaret became victim to a story that
became a folklore on the rez, but no one looked at the
origin of Susan's demise, nor the church's creative cover-ups

Laila

remembered
the night you painted
the world in shades of beer

afraid of the mother
who lived within you
singing

god didn't make honky-tonk angels
terrifying possibilities
drunk-pushing women

to the edge
of their beating hearts
yours, intoxicated yellow

it was something
beyond your skin
and you cried spineless

and it was something
Laila never forgot
moving forward

When Yellow Leaves Detach

after all, he was a childless uncle
arriving on the west coast from Winnipeg
bent on spoiling his only sister's children
she left this world for the unknown

ravens and crows speckled trees
on the way to Port Moody
it was the time of year when yellow leaves detach
he understood all things beautiful must die

he entered a dead woman's home
arms overflowing with ungrateful gifts
expecting graciousness from strangers
he heard a crow caw as the door closed

alone with children he didn't know
small talk was thick and oily with grief
coffee dripped along the wall of his cup
he sipped away sweet blackness

parenthood was not what he imagined
the ambiance was as cold as the Red River
full of Indigenous women's bodies
his dumbfounded heart caught in the undercurrents

he thought about the *North End Love Songs*
momentarily transitioned to Katherena Vermette
wishing he was a woman birthing
he would know something then

Dad

never speak ill of the dead

dad told me
they are now ancestors

and they hear soft words

be kind
before you become one of them

I have a lot to learn

Adam

used the bible
to create codes
that embodied
every sound
embedded
in Secwepemctsín
to keep alive
what the ancestors
had left him

this was redemption

Zach

told me
his story
once again
drawing me
into his
addictions
so that
I will never
forget
addictions
are cunning

Albert

never forgot
hard work virtue
deeply valued
by the Secwépemc

he toiled
endlessly, for the sake of others
without complaints
without wants

after leaving
his ten-year stay at KIRS
a protégé of brother shirley
his every move was premeditated

this was his survival
and the rez boys were keen
to his unyielding motives
because they knew brother shirley all too well

George

George's soul awakened
in the night long and cold

he exchanged stories in darkness
expelling myths of boys and girls

never to become fathers or mothers
never to return home

he saw the dreary skeletons
protruding from orchard floors

the bones buried in mortar
walls keeping secrets

he was ghosted by footsteps
echoing dull yellow corridors

carrying spectral rhythms
along paths leading to apple blossoms

where wild branches intertwined
like tangled arms crawling at the living

decade upon decade
struggling to keep names alive

reminding him in deep winter
he was the voice for the departed

Angus

dreamed of love on starlit nights
when bones of crows crawled
across his bedroom walls
making shadows

no one taught him
that he was born clean
that crows don't live a long life
that dreams are reflections

but he learned his nakedness
caused trepidation for dying crows
destined to become skeletons
piled high in the pope's cemetery

undaunting, his dreams were cyclic
envisioning things in shades of grey
until love became an array of rainbow colours
it was then, shadows became forms

Michael

attacked
his own kin

who were the marks
of lateral violence

backs against backs
weight in double life

imperceptive strikes
longing escape

potent disturbance displayed
tragically over social media

foul messages puked out
making a mess on facebook

his null-set mind digging up bones
ridiculing lives thriving on disparity

he was heartless
scorning others

intoxicated by complicit tears
shard optimism ending the day

still, kin sat at the 215 monument
resounding the weight of hope

ears acclimatized to the sound of silence
hearts immune to further strikes

Andrew

was mountain raised
never saw a white man
until that day on the rez
when visiting relatives

he heard wailing
knew death was near
shepherded by men
wearing black dresses
pointing bony fingers
towards cattle trucks
choosing children
for internment
at the KIRS death camp

unaware of the inferno
that lay ahead
he full-heartedly trusted ancestors
imploring them
across Secwepemcúlucw
vowing to remain
Secwépemc
bringing to life
the memory of 'the missing'
to be become known
as *le estcwicwéy̓*

this was his revenge

Bobby

repelled by the stink of priests
swore
that liquor would never
pass his lips
knowing the stench of men
were bayonets pricking boys'
bodies on drunk nights

he understood
judgment was for the dead
and found strength in forgiving
his perpetrators' narcissism
after all, freedom is self-love

this was an act of renewal

Timmy

peered
out of a school dorm
window on a January day
drawn into wind gusts
swiping snow tuffs
off of fragile twigs
airborne like diamonds bursting

he remembered
the rez, riding horseback in winter
his pony crushing January snow
the sound echoing sharp songs
flurries fluttering from the silver sky
melting from body heat
scarecrows stood frozen in fields
he rode on home

he recalled
his mom's beauty in natural form
bannock and deer soup atop the stove
his dad's kind eyes and quiet strength
telling stories around the kitchen table
his voice, a meadowlark's flawless song
lulling him into the long days of summer
when the sun touched his skin
and the land was full and ripe

he lingered in memory
rich and pure long-gone dreams
wishing he was home
wishing for freedom on January days

Clem

drank himself into sobriety
fifty years in the making

pierced with KIRS guilt
hurting too much to count

he spun
a drunkard's war cry

arrows protruding
from his heart and fists

cycles of addiction
and repetitive entrapment

caused him to plummet
where rocks don't break

the shock of it drove him to
compassion for other brown-skinned kin

not even Jesus could compete with that
Clem was a true saviour

Eric

discovered
not all disasters
make news

for example, he used
his voice to teach
that the white majority
was the voice
of the brown minority

breaking news

Cody

knew who he was
true to his mother's Secwépemc soul
devoted to his father's Stó:lō heart

an artist and athlete
solid in mind and body
the perfect colonial prospect

capturing the Canadian eye
drawing in neurotic diversity desires
expounding the ethnic stereotype

he dwelled as an old soul
thriving in white desires
simply dismissing settler thickness

Cam

thinks
he's losing
him to a world
he cannot see

but he is standing
clearly in open sight
bold and grounded
strange, thoughts are illusive

Ryan

knew every Fox and Kiyoti
story spun from uncle's heart
each story living in his fibres
because he escaped KIRS

uncle saw the ancestors
live in Ryan
his raw heart beating
rhythmic thumping
drumming life-song
more ancient than words
yipped from Fox's throat

Ryan's old soul fox-trotted
down a path a thousand years
in the making, finding a way
to Kiyoti's den, plain and simple
clean and pure synchronization

who would've thought
Kiyoti would weep from Ryan's throat
instead of howling
when he saw
Fox with love eyes?

Ryan was told that Fox
had the power to bring
Kiyoti back to natural life
and perhaps it's true
his raw heart beats forevermore
uncle saw it coming

Boyd

was most alive at dusk
when the summer skies swiveled
sweating warm showers

he lay naked
beneath shifting clouds
soaking in possibilities

sweet trickling rain
wetting his tongue and body
in natural discourse

sacred embodiment
that his ancestors knew
sinking into sunset

Gus

could not be captured for long
he escaped the residential school
one month after imprisonment

he said he sang
his spirit back to the *Horse People*
who helped him gallop away without sound

he told the story many times
inspiring others tsqelmucwílc
'to return to being human again'

Darcy

walked, like many other young people,
trance-like down black roads
needles dangling from his arm
spoons boiling death crack – crack!
liquor sizzling his liver
yellow skin aching red
intergenerational trauma
clotting minds
building tent cities on East Hastings
far removed from soft rain on a rez

granny and grampa, like the Old Ones, lament
outliving the youth
dull knives carving ditches on old faces
frozen in terror
doubting they did the right thing
by KIRS stories of struggle and survival
hearts barely pumping love anymore
afraid of what a new day might bring
scrambling in the chaos of hope
this world has gone crazy
Darcy disappeared into a dark road

Henry

was cruel, and obsessed
with being deviant, he was
a barn-worker at KIRS
and knew animals well
brother shirley taught him everything
about vindictiveness to animals and children

when he was discovered
they cut the animal out of him

Joe

Joe's KIRS beatings
died
each time the drum came
alive

when he sang Indian blues
pounding
from the depths of his marrow
insistently

songs kept coming to him
relentlessly
breathy spirits channelled through him
unapologetically

after all, Joe was Secwépemc
deeply
Secwepémc wel me7 yéws
Secwepémc wel me7 yéws

Keegan

asked black questions
knowing it was a dangerous hunt

ready
for ambiguous answers

he filtered
manipulation easily

whiskey scorn intuition
kept things real for him at all costs

street life depended on it
dull deception was obvious

he learned this well
secrets hold deadly consequences

so he said, "don't ask
unless you are willing to pay the price"

and don't hunt
unless you are willing to kill

John

altar boy, John, the handsome one
father's pale favourite
cleansed wine chalices
where priests prowled
after Sunday mass, choking John
on his cock and cheap wine

they said "John's mouth
was stuffed so full of death,
he died starving"

Elijah

it was a forsaken sunset
watching him disappear
along a path well-worn
leading away from apple orchards
piled high with ditched skeletons
barely alive in memory

red and black clouds
stretched across the long horizon
wisps of wind promising sky-tears
filling his soul with freshness,
the scent of earth after it rains
were bees buzzing in his belly
was like finding love in utter sorrow

his constricting grief
and low self-worth was hatched
in residential school dorms
as he prayed on callused knees
accompanied by god's men
laying naked on white sheets
a finger beckoning arousal calls

despite his tender soul
craving life and love
he found a path to walk
leading into forever
obscurity
and these were his last steps
walking down lover's lane
holding hands with himself

Kenny

hung from the end
of a rope in the KIRS barn
swinging from burnt rafters
cows regurgitating
what priests sewed below

his purple face swollen
his eyes bulging bewilderment
his chest stuck in shame and grief

at his funeral, the priest said
"Jesus hung from a cross"
there was no mention of Kenny
for us to remember
but that rope still hangs there – bodiless

Lucas

understood if his heart was breaking
Violet's must be too

neither of them built those
indiscernible walls

forcing brother and sister apart
forbidden to be family at KIRS

told that their love was dirty
and their names were savage and filthy

if they were to shatter that barrier
scars would become another fortification

fragments of glass
traveling in their blood streams

divesting kinship
by unnatural design

broke his heart
lugging it to the grave

waiting his turn
to greet Violet on the other side

Nels

lived in scars
believing
wounds heal

Millie sang him back
to the drum
where he thrived
on the skin of deer

returning to being human again
his voice grew from the land
dissipating disfigurements

cousins fully alive
locked in unbreakable ties
singing, dancing land memory
KIRS was no match for them

Peter

protected us
fiercely, sharp with words
if we tried to wander
off unaccompanied
to use the washroom
in the basement at KIRS

"never go pee alone,
brother shirley lurks"
he warned because that monk
trolled and preyed on boys
naïve to the pricks in the world

I wish I had listened to him

Robert

fog formed in Robert's eyes
the day he told
the story of his missing
three fingers
cut off at the joints
because he was a thief
stealing food
for starving kids
at the residential school

he has learned to live
without them, all of them

Maverick

arrived dressed in death
and stood by your side
while you lay still
like a spiritless, caged sparrow
in room 215, bare essentials
supporting you
machines rhythmically
dreaming up hope
fluids flowing along plastic creeks
seeping into your sleeping arm
hospital rooms tick away time
measure the weight of a man's life in seconds
he stared
remembering you at a different time

you did not flinch
to neither his presence
nor to the insistent humming
of life-support equipment
overpowering the silence
but your eyes rolled in dreamland
concocting hope
but innately aware of mortality
smelling it everywhere
amid hospital corridors
lingering in a mixture of tasteless food
and lifeless grey skin
awaiting to leave this world to the unknown
nothing more aroused your hunger

it was then, he understood
faith runs away in terror
hides behind the windows of priests
who hide from their own deeds
and who are stubbornly afraid
to open curtains letting in the sun
allowing its power to shine

and warm the dying faces of men

but he lived
through the brutality of residential schools
dirty love
displacement
torn apart families
alcoholism
and every trauma
known to the human flesh and soul

he could only weep
when you yelled
"I hate you
I hate you
I hate you,
residential school"

and now, in your grey silence
your stillness speaks boldly
telling you that he is ready
to greet an experience he will one day have
and forcing him to relive the trepidation
so easily concealed in someone else's sorrow

Maverick turned
and walked towards the open door
never looking back

imagining the good times
he stood at your grave
forsaken

Sanjiv

in my days adrift,
I could not have imagined you
bringing back to life
euphoric chimes
tucked deeply within my soul's fibres
but there you were
in the white sound of city noise
standing at my doorstep
softly lipping
the mystery of love lyrics
enticing me to ocean's edge
tasting the sea's salt
and walking amid
shadows of men with no names
sunlight shrouding you
touching my withered skin
bringing back to life
my barely beating heart
the song's whispers
quelling my cravings
and I heard
ice melting in me
opening breath to new air
my pounding pulse pumping
a new chance
a new beginning
swimming and thriving
within your immortal name – Sanjiv
and each time I exhaled
I was further revived
seeing transformation before me
seeing Fox, the revivor, the dreamer
dreaming
a thousand times recurring
a thousand years reincarnated
cupping my bent spirit
Sanjiv's soul

so gentle, so soft

how could I not fall in love?

Tapéte

worked amid cacti and weeds
overtaking tspenpén – the graveyard

often drunk among the dead
but eternally respectful

he knew ancestors
and reminded us

stories reinforce our identity
tens of thousands of years old

we are here
because of our ancestors

"I survived
knowing their stories," he said

I wish I had listened more closely

Garry

read me love poems

wanted January Marie Rogers
whispering raspy, breathy poetry

wanted Pablo Neruda
swimming in his words

wanted Karlo Mila
undressing love-shame

wanted Jimmy Baca
heaving in my chest

wanted Joy Harjo
releasing his name

wanted Billy-Ray Belcourt
setting me abound

wanted me
215 words at a time

read me love poems

The Vatican

no
one is born in the vatican
barring
accident

codes
of silence are sealed weapons
where popes are beyond
law

there
exists hierarchies of priesthood
much lower than angels but active whores of
devils

mercenaries
of desire and deceit
protected in the house of
god

cardinals
and condoms are disposable
at the holy man's will on this side of
heaven

bastards
born from the disorder of affections
spawn torrid romances and sordid
tales

secretly
alive beneath black and white cloth
bodies and rooms full of terrorized
silence

Father Alan

his relentless weapon
sought moist pits

purple power jetting
an uncontrollable deprivation

his instinctive appetite
heavenly thwarted

not necessarily by choice
but by the code of canon law

forcing synthetic redemption
solving the problem

swirling his tongue into
sloppy prayer

rosaries skinning his hands
bleeding out his sins

dripping blood onto his targets
innocent souls

surviving rusty memories
cursing the church

cursing a blistered pope
angry at the world

crossing lines
between innocence and sin

this
was his calling

Father John

leaned against Jesus' chest
at the last supper
the love of his life

his pain was the lord's pain
how quickly things die
when permission is granted

father john pulled himself
out of pages in the bible
and reinvented himself

filling catholic rooms
with pungent scent
as the silent moons wept

wild sweat thickening air
lingering in hallways
the windows closed

his barbed face burning
anticipation
crossing that line habitually

Jesus was not at his chest anymore
but there lay children beneath him
learning to die in moments like this

dropping to his knees
for any saviour are lessons
never to be forgotten

and knowing god's son
died for irrational reasoning
quickly dried his bloodshot eyes

he did his unholy deeds

behind walls built for him
in rooms used for bleeding

knowing scars are forever
reminders stark in daylight
and numb to catechism teachings

flogging became an existential turn on
since redemption was careless dreaming
perhaps he was an atheist after all

Brother Shirley

had thin
blue eyes
narrow long lips
sharp
cheekbones

his speckled
red
moving parts
draped in black cloth
indicative of shapeshifters

he had
tall devil desires
calculated with precision
along the right angles
of dungy corridors
preying on boys
needing to piss release

his release
was calculatingly repetitive
discharged in the private
places of boys

his victims
were far from
manhood knowing
and voiceless among oblate men
consecrated by church and god

he vowed
poverty and obedience
but was proficient
in the pedagogy of the oppressed

his secrets

set his skin on fire
when the sun bowed west

he avoided
bibles and confession box conversations
sitting alone at the last supper table
where more sins were secretly born

his instinctiveness
making its way
to sharp ears and active minds
entrenched in the malaise of celibacy

his thin
blue eyes
tracing
the naked form of faultless boys
slaughter without penalty

Sister Superior

moved gracefully
descending chapel steps
a butterfly walk
fluttering stairwells
and corridors and rez
school hallways, angel-like
beauty among lords
a slight head bow
a Marilyn Monroe smile
adored by contemporaries
feared by the sad-eyed rez kids
obedient to her whims and anger

she was the lily in Jesus' hand
as they marched to death
on orchard trails leading west
a quirt dangling from her wrist
swinging in perfect harmony
with the beads and crucifix tied
seductively waist height
accentuating chastity long gone

her angelic whispers
weakened the knees
of priests, monks and nuns alike
obsessed with divine intervention
thick-headed to the true will of god
bent on genocidal reform

she killed
in the most beautiful way
never forgotten

Sister Mary Bernadette

taught cruelty in grade three
rather than arithmetic
or how to read things clearly

her magnified eyes
overtook the classroom
endlessly searching for flaws

and without fail
she found imperfections
at the edge of her skin

wielding a pink strap
exerting pride and privilege
coerced upon the innocent

she impaled harmless spirits
vigorously teaching them
pain ends in the loop of a rope

she crucified students
stacked bibles upon bleeding palms
nailed her sins to every page

prayed enthusiastically
that the Indian in them
would die with each drop of blood

she abstained from funerals
kept nooses for trophies
believed they would save her

but her methods failed
as she rotted in hell
dumping her original calling

Sister Mary Charles Anthony

if there was
if there was

such a thing
such a thing

as kindness
as kindness

at KIRS
at KIRS

then it subsisted
then it subsisted

in Sister Mary Charles Anthony
in Sister Mary Charles Anthony

God's Shame

the queen and pope's mercenaries
used children's souls as bullets
aimed at the hearts of parents
execution style
without disgrace

an act of charity, they claimed
orders of a civilized society
construed at buckingham palace
and within the pope's bedroom
premeditating genocide

let's call it what it really is
in the name of *terra nullius*
the devil's greed
god's shame
a queen's victory

Speak Ill of Us

we cannot speak ill of the dead
nor blame the ancestors
because we have jeered
away from cultural purity

we are here
because of those who once lived
and left us with the land's language
steeped deeply within the soul's fibre
and it is not ours to alter, but to keep simply
for those yet to be born

there is a danger in
accepting colonial constructs
forming new identities
centred around superiority and inferiority
racist practices
internalized racism
gender classification
all perpetuating state ward mentality

brown cannot become the new white
otherwise, those of the future will
not be able to name that new colour
and will speak ill of us
once we are ancestors

You

clung to stories of Latino conquest
swirling at the centre
edgy characters in love and war
caught in your heart

rosaries swinging from mixed-blood necks
timely in prayer – the lord's prayer
tattooed on sweat-dripping chests
protecting what lurks honestly in guts
eyes elongated over southern oceans
stretching and landing on the Salish Sea,
the perfect setting for a perfect climax
drawn between quest and passion
embedded in the bodies of Latino men

the world must know
fireworks in the dark places of bodies
releasing a kaleidoscope of colour
blanketing the blue of a midnight sky
a continuation of sounds and colours flash-dancing
crimson and lime green particles of clothing
strobing, fluttering in English Bay dimness on sand

the explosion causing cravings of chocolate ice-cream
and the many things that churn beneath one's skin
leading to booming kisses erupting
and blending a fusion of defeat and delight
taming bodily addictions – a heart's scorn
heard in the background
murmurings strangers
amid the calligraphy of clouds

it was an El Salvadorian night never to be forgotten
webbed by characters fluttering in firework sparks
dissolving into the belly of a July night

I

uncannily
brew
transition
like a runaway buck
torn between
the safety of the forest
and paved roads
baring city streets
teeming wild animals
escaping zoos

I am charmed
by danger
dodging entrapment
and game for excitement
an aimed bullet
pointing at my heart
a knife at my jugular
staring at you in the eye
you are not
so ominous

I am crazy
with elation
scowls
bouncing
from the roof of my mouth
spewing
whimsical turmoil
confusing
your essence
weaving
guttural rutting songs
charismatic melodies
you cannot kill

I am dangerously
alluring
in autumn
scraping horns
on aspens
grunting near
sweet springs and salt licks

my lifeblood
taking in
the brisk fall air
aware
of your musky scent
lingering on aspen bark

I am fine-tuned
in natural space
but a lunatic
in confinement

I am vigilant…
the on-coming winter
thickens my skin
stings my bones
my back bent to the south
my keen body
my alert ears
ready for the slightest sound
sharp to the hunter's pounding heart
zoned in on the twitching finger
caressing the trigger

I am fearless
knowing
that you have schooled me
well in death
astute
that ecstasy is living fully

I see
the open sights
the crossroads that lay ahead
and I know
my path is clear

We

lay awake
aching for home
this dorm is thick
dry grief choking
disparity
smashing bricks
plank floors echoing
midnight steps

Kiyoti numbs the body
plays mind tricks
but Father Alan keeps
sounds real
beating down
resistance
one by one

we comply
follow him to his bed
and then to the orchard

robotic silence
shovels and picks
smashing down on rocks
softening dense clay
215 more to go
our bodies ache
rain

About the Author

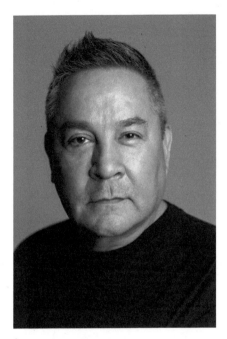

PHOTO FARAH NOSH

Garry Gottfriedson, B.Ed., M.A.Ed., LLD h.c., is from Kamloops, BC. He is strongly rooted in his Secwepémc cultural teachings. He holds a Master of Education Degree from Simon Fraser University. Gottfriedson also achieved an Honorary Doctor of Laws from the University of Northern British Columbia and a Doctor of Letters from Thompson Rivers University. In 1987, the Naropa Institute in Boulder, Colorado, awarded a Creative Writing Scholarship to Gottfriedson for Master of Fine Arts in Creative Writing. There, he studied under Allen Ginsberg, Marianne Faithfull and others. Gottfriedson has thirteen published books. He has read from his work across Canada, the United States, South America, New Zealand, Europe, and Asia. Gottfriedson's work unapologetically unveils the truth of Canada's treatment of First Nations. His work has been anthologized and published nationally and internationally.